I0559149

DOODLE & DREAM

Student Success Activity Book

AGES 9+

THIS BOOK BELONGS TO

_____

FAVORITE SHOW

_____

FAVORITE SONG

_____

PHONE #

_____

STEPHANIE RUIZ MALONE

This book was created to help guide you through your journey as a student. At times situations can be frustrating, annoying, and hurtful, but the key to getting through tough times is to motivate yourself and push forward toward your goals..

Don't know exactly what those goals are? It's okay some reveal themselves immediately and others reveal themselves with time. The activities within these pages will help you process your thoughts and feelings in fun, creative ways to help you achieve your dreams!

****

It's hard to be perfect and mistake-free all the time. Try not to compare yourself to others. Everyone reaches their goals and dreams at different times. Do the best you can do right now. Your hard work will lead you to exactly where you need to be. I'm so excited about all the wonderful things I know you will accomplish this school year. Keep shining your light!

****

Thank you so much for choosing this activity book!

I'd love to know how it has transformed your student journey. I value your honest review and look forward to hearing your thoughts. Subscribe to the Estrella Brillante newsletter for future product releases and year-round motivation and inspiration, For easy access, scan the QR code below:

Free mini motivational poster download with sign-up

****

Created for you with ♥
Stephanie Ruiz Malone

ISBN: 979-8-9882808-5-9

9 798988 280859

THIS IS WHERE THE JOURNEY BEGINS!

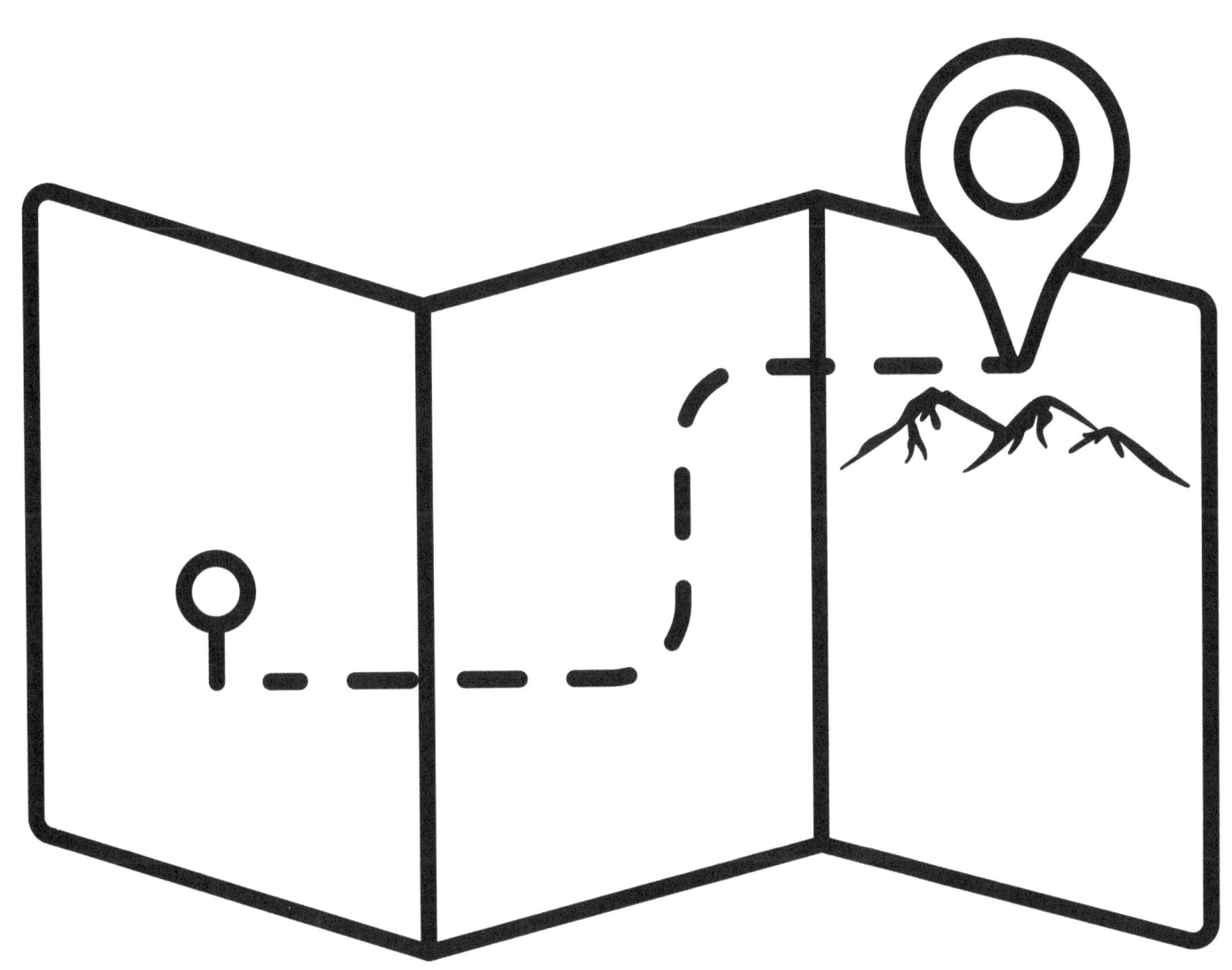

IMAGINE THE

POSSIBILITIES...

Idea Board

COVER WITH STICKERS, CLIPPINGS, ETC.

"I can make positive things happen."

My Dreams

Draw or write your dreams or future goals within the clouds

DOODLES

_____

WEEK

I'm grateful for...

♡

♡

♡

♡

Top 3 Goals

◯ _____

◯ _____

◯ _____

To- Do List

☐ _____

☐ _____

☐ _____

☐ _____

☐ _____

☐ _____

☐ _____

☐ _____

Take a deep breath, you've got this!

WEEK _____

I'm grateful for...

♡ _____

♡ _____

♡ _____

♡ _____

Top 3 Goals

○ _____

○ _____

○ _____

To- Do List

☐ _____
☐ _____
☐ _____
☐ _____
☐ _____
☐ _____
☐ _____
☐ _____

Take a deep breath, you've got this!

_____ WEEK

I'm grateful for ...

♡

♡

♡

♡

Top 3 Goals

○ _____

○ _____

○ _____

To- Do List

☐ _____

☐ _____

☐ _____

☐ _____

☐ _____

☐ _____

☐ _____

☐ _____

Take a deep breath, you've got this!

_____

WEEK

I'm grateful for...

♡

♡

♡

♡

Top 3 Goals

○ _____

○ _____

○ _____

To- Do List

☐ _____

☐ _____

☐ _____

☐ _____

☐ _____

☐ _____

☐ _____

☐ _____

Take a deep breath, you've got this!

YOU'VE
GOT THIS!
KEEP
GOING!

Idea Board

COVER WITH STICKERS, CLIPPINGS, ETC.

My Icons

Draw any images that represent you!

 # DOODLES

_____

WEEK

I'm grateful for...

♡

♡

♡

♡

Top 3 Goals

○ _____

○ _____

○ _____

To- Do List

☐ _____

☐ _____

☐ _____

☐ _____

☐ _____

☐ _____

☐ _____

☐ _____

Take a deep breath, you've got this!

_____ WEEK

I'm grateful for...

♡

♡

♡

♡

Top 3 Goals

○ _____

○ _____

○ _____

To- Do List

☐ _____

☐ _____

☐ _____

☐ _____

☐ _____

☐ _____

☐ _____

☐ _____

Take a deep breath, you've got this!

_____

WEEK

I'm grateful for...

♡

♡

♡

♡

Top 3 Goals

○ _____

○ _____

○ _____

To- Do List

☐ _____

☐ _____

☐ _____

☐ _____

☐ _____

☐ _____

☐ _____

☐ _____

Take a deep breath, you've got this!

_____ WEEK

I'm grateful for...

♡

♡

♡

♡

Top 3 Goals

◯ _____

◯ _____

◯ _____

To- Do List

☐ _____

☐ _____

☐ _____

☐ _____

☐ _____

☐ _____

☐ _____

☐ _____

Take a deep breath, you've got this!

THE JOURNEY MAY BE LONG, BUT IT'S TOTALLY WORTH IT.

Idea Board

COVER WITH STICKERS, CLIPPINGS, ETC.

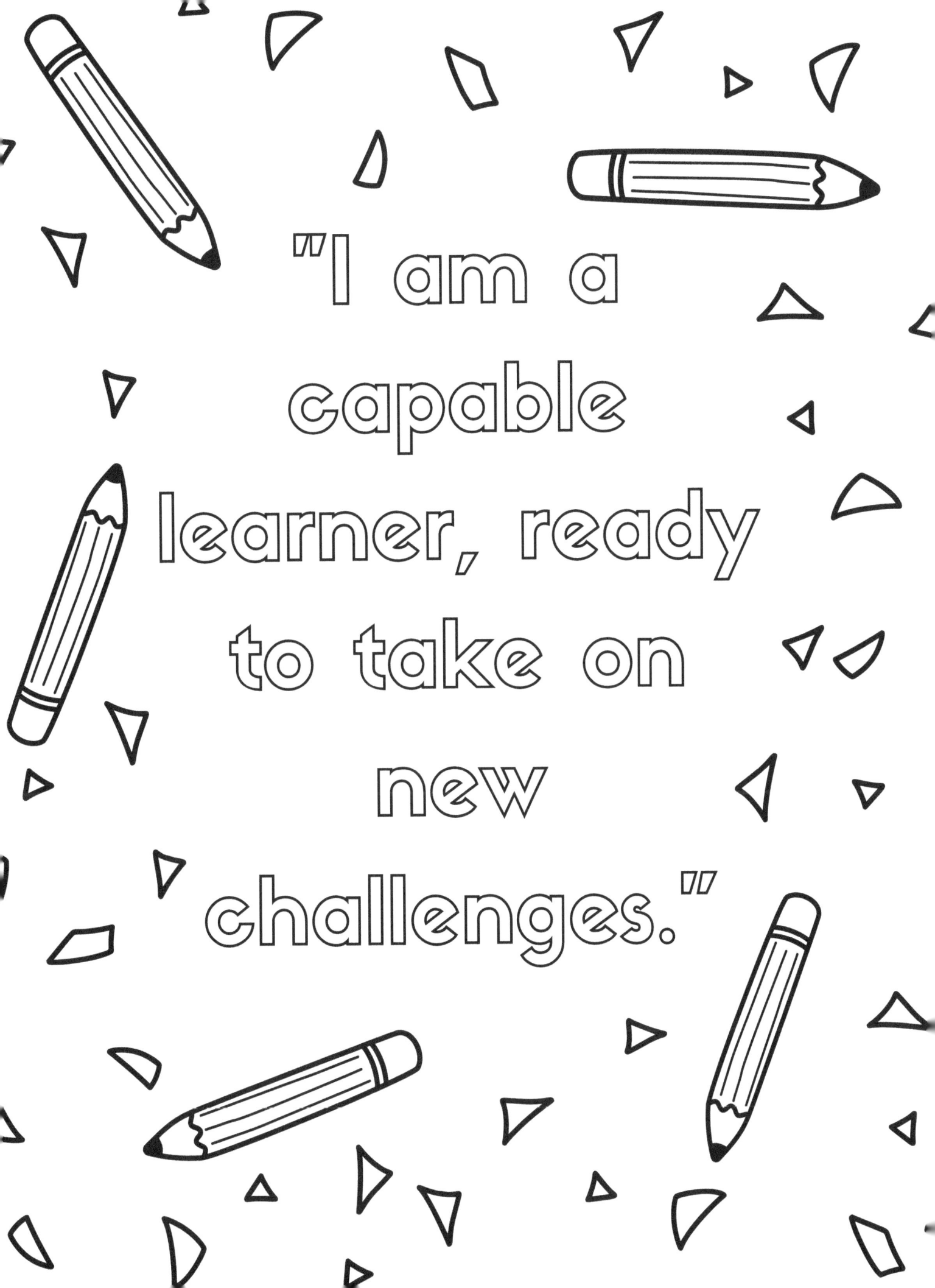

"I am a capable learner, ready to take on new challenges."

My Ultimate Goal

_____
_____
_____
_____

_____
_____
_____
_____
_____
_____
_____

What do you need to do to climb the mountain and reach your goal(s)?

_____
_____
_____
_____

DOODLES

_____

WEEK

I'm grateful for ...

♡

♡

♡

♡

Top 3 Goals

○ _____

○ _____

○ _____

To- Do List

☐ _____

☐ _____

☐ _____

☐ _____

☐ _____

☐ _____

☐ _____

☐ _____

Take a deep breath, you've got this!

WEEK ___

I'm grateful for...

♡ _____

♡ _____

♡ _____

♡ _____

Top 3 Goals

○ _____

○ _____

○ _____

To- Do List

☐ _____

☐ _____

☐ _____

☐ _____

☐ _____

☐ _____

☐ _____

☐ _____

Take a deep breath, you've got this!

_____

WEEK

I'm grateful for...

♡

♡

♡

♡

Top 3 Goals

○ _____

○ _____

○ _____

To- Do List

☐ _____

☐ _____

☐ _____

☐ _____

☐ _____

☐ _____

☐ _____

☐ _____

Take a deep breath, you've got this!

_____

WEEK

I'm grateful for...

♡

♡

♡

♡

Top 3 Goals

◯ _____

◯ _____

◯ _____

To- Do List

☐ _____

☐ _____

☐ _____

☐ _____

☐ _____

☐ _____

☐ _____

☐ _____

Take a deep breath, you've got this!

LEARNING FROM MISTAKES IS THE KEY TO SUCCESS!

Idea Board

COVER WITH STICKERS, CLIPPINGS, ETC.

My life
journey
so far....

 # DOODLES

_____

WEEK

I'm grateful for ...

♡

♡

♡

♡

Top 3 Goals

○ _____

○ _____

○ _____

To- Do List

☐ _____
☐ _____
☐ _____
☐ _____
☐ _____
☐ _____
☐ _____
☐ _____

Take a deep breath, you've got this!

_____

WEEK

I'm grateful for...

♡

♡

♡

♡

Top 3 Goals

○ _____

○ _____

○ _____

To- Do List

☐ _____

☐ _____

☐ _____

☐ _____

☐ _____

☐ _____

☐ _____

☐ _____

Take a deep breath, you've got this!

_____

WEEK

I'm grateful for...

♡

♡

♡

♡

Top 3 Goals

○ _____

○ _____

○ _____

To- Do List

☐ _____

☐ _____

☐ _____

☐ _____

☐ _____

☐ _____

☐ _____

☐ _____

Take a deep breath, you've got this!

WEEK

I'm grateful for...

♡

♡

♡

♡

Top 3 Goals

○ _____

○ _____

○ _____

To- Do List

☐ _____

☐ _____

☐ _____

☐ _____

☐ _____

☐ _____

☐ _____

☐ _____

Take a deep breath, you've got this!

PUSH THROUGH THE FEAR OF THE UNKNOWN:

☆ YOU ARE NEVER ALONE.

☆ YOU WILL EVOLVE INTO THE PERSON YOU WANT TO BE.

Idea Board

COVER WITH STICKERS, CLIPPINGS, ETC.

What makes your heart happy?

Draw/write anything that brings you happiness.

 # DOODLES

_____

WEEK

I'm grateful for...

♡

♡

♡

♡

Top 3 Goals

○ _____

○ _____

○ _____

To- Do List

☐ _____
☐ _____
☐ _____
☐ _____
☐ _____
☐ _____
☐ _____
☐ _____

Take a deep breath, you've got this!

_____
WEEK

I'm grateful for...

♡

♡

♡

♡

Top 3 Goals

○ _____

○ _____

○ _____

To- Do List

☐ _____
☐ _____
☐ _____
☐ _____
☐ _____
☐ _____
☐ _____
☐ _____

Take a deep breath, you've got this!

_____
WEEK

I'm grateful for ...

♡

♡

♡

♡

Top 3 Goals

○ _____

○ _____

○ _____

To- Do List

☐ _____

☐ _____

☐ _____

☐ _____

☐ _____

☐ _____

☐ _____

☐ _____

Take a deep breath, you've got this!

WEEK _____

I'm grateful for...

♡ _____

♡ _____

♡ _____

♡ _____

Top 3 Goals

○ _____

○ _____

○ _____

To- Do List

☐ _____

☐ _____

☐ _____

☐ _____

☐ _____

☐ _____

☐ _____

☐ _____

Take a deep breath, you've got this!

IT'S OKAY TO TAKE A BREAK AND RETURN WITH FRESH EYES!

Idea Board

COVER WITH STICKERS, CLIPPINGS, ETC.

Fill the sunrays with your thoughts.

I am grateful for...

 # DOODLES

WEEK

I'm grateful for...

♡

♡

♡

♡

Top 3 Goals

○ _____

○ _____

○ _____

To- Do List

☐ _____

☐ _____

☐ _____

☐ _____

☐ _____

☐ _____

☐ _____

☐ _____

Take a deep breath, you've got this!

WEEK

I'm grateful for...

♡

♡

♡

♡

Top 3 Goals

○ _____

○ _____

○ _____

To- Do List

☐ _____

☐ _____

☐ _____

☐ _____

☐ _____

☐ _____

☐ _____

☐ _____

Take a deep breath, you've got this!

_____

WEEK

I'm grateful for...

♡

♡

♡

♡

Top 3 Goals

○ _____

○ _____

○ _____

To- Do List

☐ _____

☐ _____

☐ _____

☐ _____

☐ _____

☐ _____

☐ _____

☐ _____

Take a deep breath, you've got this!

_____

WEEK

I'm grateful for...

♡

♡

♡

♡

Top 3 Goals

◯ _____

◯ _____

◯ _____

To- Do List

☐ _____

☐ _____

☐ _____

☐ _____

☐ _____

☐ _____

☐ _____

☐ _____

Take a deep breath, you've got this!

TAKE IT A DAY AT A TIME, ALL WILL WORK ITSELF OUT.

Idea Board

COVER WITH STICKERS, CLIPPINGS, ETC.

What inspires you to succeed?

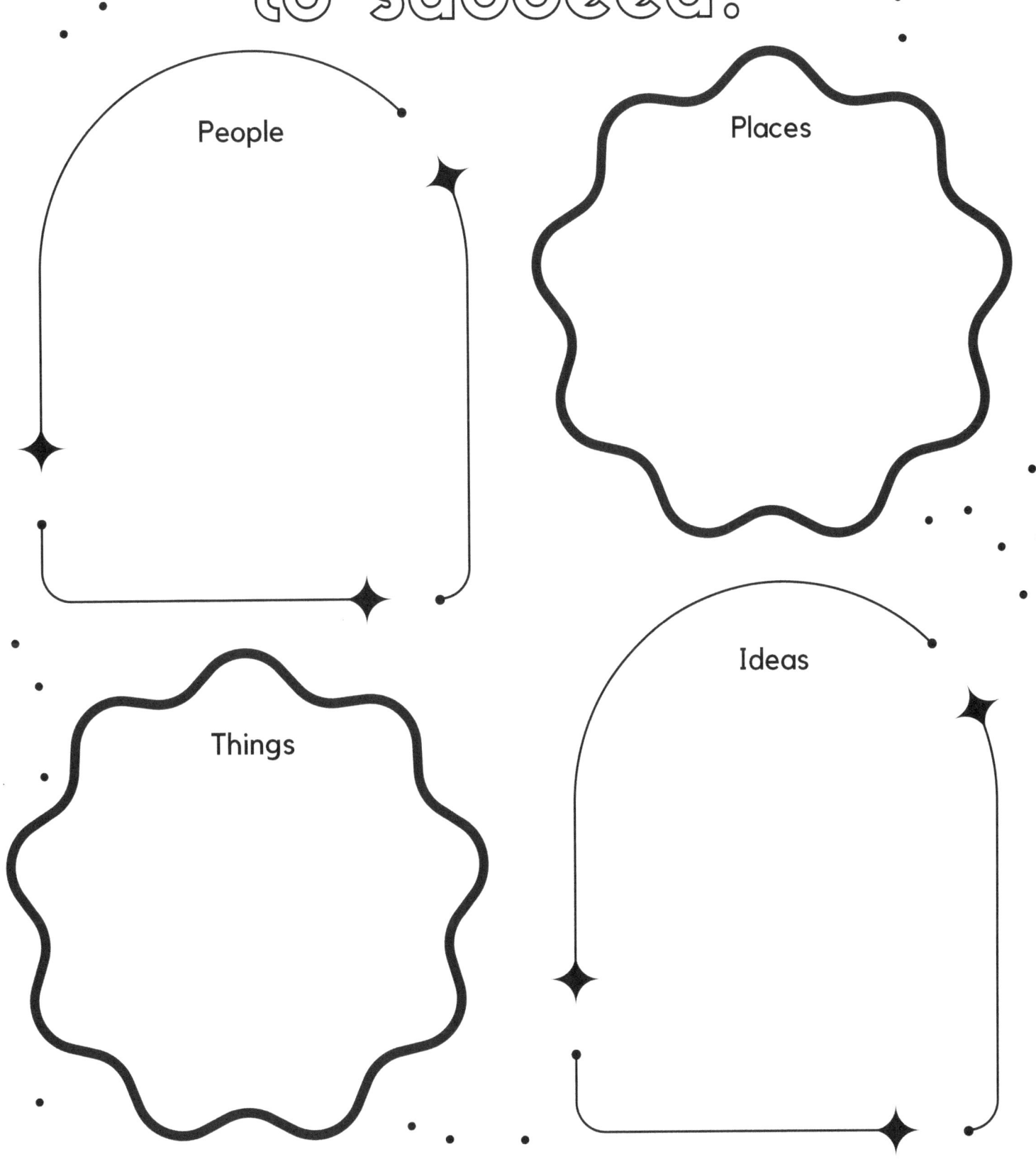

People

Places

Things

Ideas

DOODLES

_____

WEEK

I'm grateful for...

♡

♡

♡

♡

Top 3 Goals

◯ _____

◯ _____

◯ _____

To- Do List

☐ _____
☐ _____
☐ _____
☐ _____
☐ _____
☐ _____
☐ _____
☐ _____

Take a deep breath, you've got this!

WEEK

I'm grateful for...

♡

♡

♡

♡

Top 3 Goals

○ _____

○ _____

○ _____

To- Do List

☐ _____

☐ _____

☐ _____

☐ _____

☐ _____

☐ _____

☐ _____

☐ _____

Take a deep breath, you've got this!

WEEK

I'm grateful for ...

♡

♡

♡

♡

Top 3 Goals

○ _____

○ _____

○ _____

To- Do List

☐ _____
☐ _____
☐ _____
☐ _____
☐ _____
☐ _____
☐ _____
☐ _____

Take a deep breath, you've got this!

WEEK _____

I'm grateful for...

♡

♡

♡

♡

Top 3 Goals

○ _____

○ _____

○ _____

To- Do List

☐ _____

☐ _____

☐ _____

☐ _____

☐ _____

☐ _____

☐ _____

☐ _____

Take a deep breath, you've got this!

TAKE A
MOMENT
TO
BREATHE...

Idea Board

COVER WITH STICKERS, CLIPPINGS, ETC.

Ideas and Solutions

 # DOODLES

WEEK

I'm grateful for...

♡

♡

♡

♡

Top 3 Goals

○ _____

○ _____

○ _____

To- Do List

☐ _____

☐ _____

☐ _____

☐ _____

☐ _____

☐ _____

☐ _____

☐ _____

Take a deep breath, you've got this!

WEEK _____

I'm grateful for...

♡

♡

♡

♡

Top 3 Goals

○ _____

○ _____

○ _____

To- Do List

☐ _____

☐ _____

☐ _____

☐ _____

☐ _____

☐ _____

☐ _____

☐ _____

Take a deep breath, you've got this!

_____ WEEK

I'm grateful for...

♡

♡

♡

♡

Top 3 Goals

○ _____

○ _____

○ _____

To- Do List

☐ _____
☐ _____
☐ _____
☐ _____
☐ _____
☐ _____
☐ _____
☐ _____

Take a deep breath, you've got this!

_____ WEEK

I'm grateful for...

♡

♡

♡

♡

Top 3 Goals

○ _____

○ _____

○ _____

To- Do List

☐ _____

☐ _____

☐ _____

☐ _____

☐ _____

☐ _____

☐ _____

☐ _____

Take a deep breath, you've got this!

OBSTACLES CAN BLOCK YOUR WAY BUT:

 **FIND HELP**

 **MAKE A PLAN**

 **BE DETERMINED TO SUCCEED**

Idea Board

COVER WITH STICKERS, CLIPPINGS, ETC.

"I am ready and well-prepared for any test or project."

You are special.

Write your unique qualities within each star.

 # DOODLES

.

WEEK

I'm grateful for...

♡

♡

♡

♡

Top 3 Goals

○ _____

○ _____

○ _____

To- Do List

☐ _____

☐ _____

☐ _____

☐ _____

☐ _____

☐ _____

☐ _____

☐ _____

Take a deep breath, you've got this!

_____

WEEK

I'm grateful for...

♡ _____

♡ _____

♡ _____

♡ _____

Top 3 Goals

○ _____

○ _____

○ _____

To- Do List

☐ _____

☐ _____

☐ _____

☐ _____

☐ _____

☐ _____

☐ _____

☐ _____

Take a deep breath, you've got this!

_____

WEEK

I'm grateful for ...

♡

♡

♡

♡

Top 3 Goals

◯ _____

◯ _____

◯ _____

To- Do List

☐ _____

☐ _____

☐ _____

☐ _____

☐ _____

☐ _____

☐ _____

☐ _____

Take a deep breath, you've got this!

WEEK _____

I'm grateful for...

♡ _____

♡ _____

♡ _____

♡ _____

Top 3 Goals

○ _____

○ _____

○ _____

To- Do List

☐ _____

☐ _____

☐ _____

☐ _____

☐ _____

☐ _____

☐ _____

☐ _____

Take a deep breath, you've got this!

YOU'RE
ALMOST
THERE. DON'T
GIVE UP!

Idea Board

COVER WITH STICKERS, CLIPPINGS, ETC.

Success Timeline

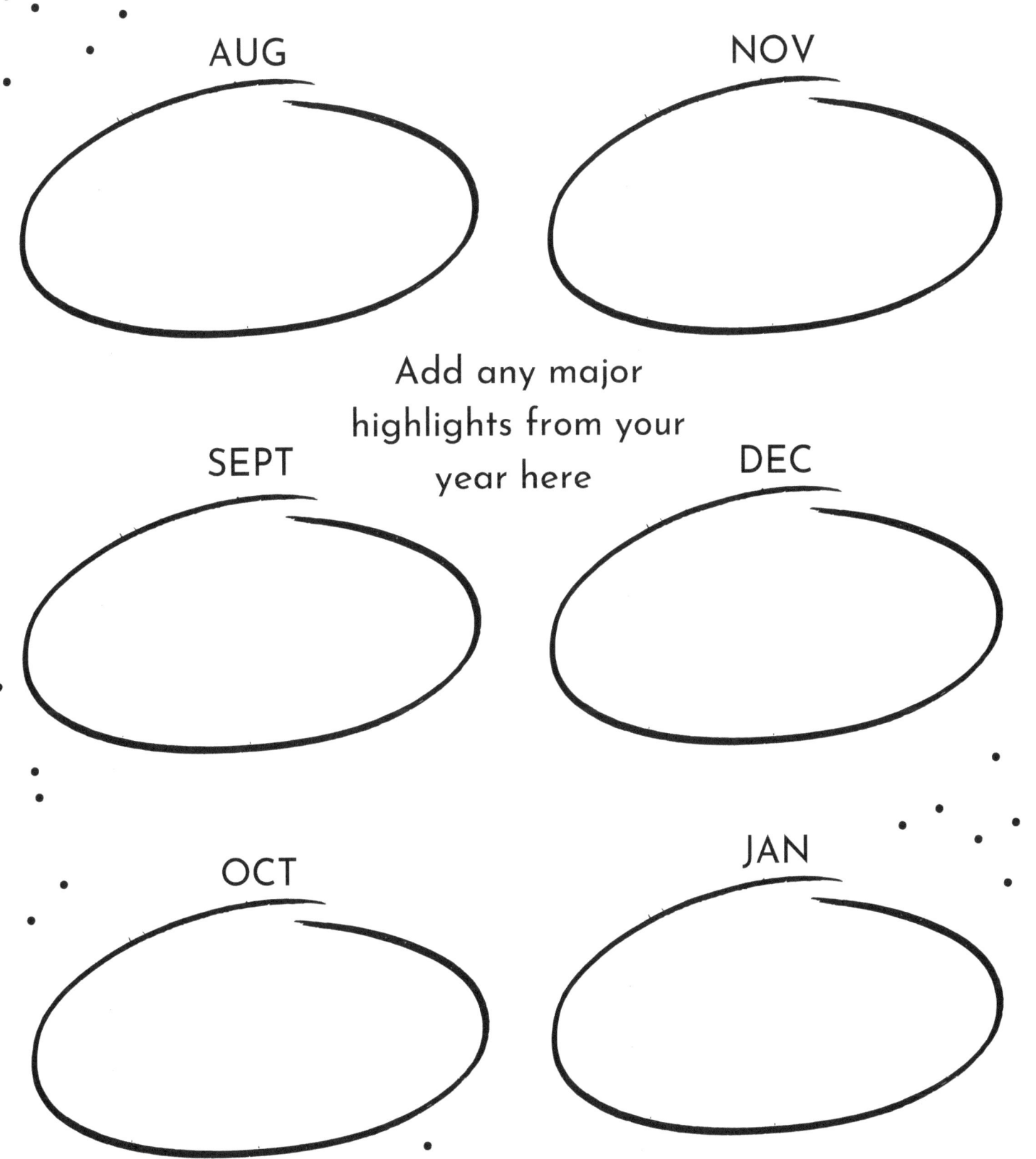

AUG

NOV

Add any major
highlights from your
year here

SEPT

DEC

OCT

JAN

Success Timeline

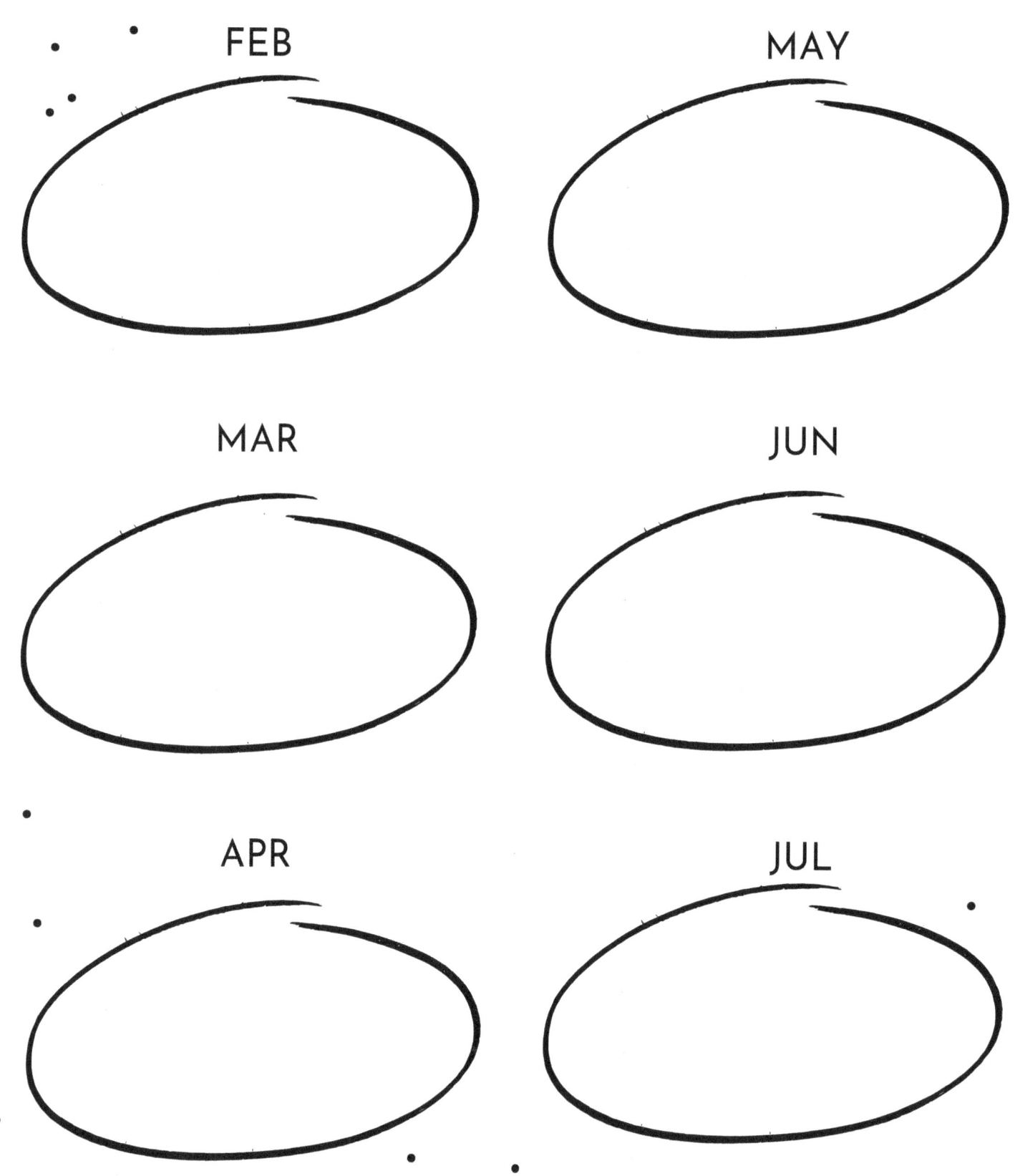

FEB

MAY

MAR

JUN

APR

JUL

 **DOODLES**

_____

WEEK

I'm grateful for ...   **Top 3 Goals**

♡   ◯ _____

♡   ◯ _____

♡   ◯ _____

♡

To- Do List

☐ _____

☐ _____

☐ _____   Take a

☐ _____   deep

☐ _____   breath,

☐ _____   you've got

☐ _____   this!

☐ _____

_____

WEEK

I'm grateful for...

♡

♡

♡

♡

Top 3 Goals

○ ——————————

○ ——————————

○ ——————————

To- Do List

☐ ——————————

☐ ——————————

☐ ——————————

☐ ——————————

☐ ——————————

☐ ——————————

☐ ——————————

☐ ——————————

Take a deep breath, you've got this!

_____ WEEK

I'm grateful for...

♡

♡

♡

♡

Top 3 Goals

○ _____

○ _____

○ _____

To- Do List

☐ _____
☐ _____
☐ _____
☐ _____
☐ _____
☐ _____
☐ _____
☐ _____

Take a deep breath, you've got this!

WEEK

I'm grateful for...

♡

♡

♡

♡

Top 3 Goals

○ _____

○ _____

○ _____

To- Do List

☐ _____

☐ _____

☐ _____

☐ _____

☐ _____

☐ _____

☐ _____

☐ _____

Take a deep breath, you've got this!

YOU MADE THE JOURNEY AND I'M SO PROUD OF YOU!

Success Board

COVER WITH STICKERS, CLIPPINGS, ETC.
RELATED TO YOUR ACHIEVEMENTS

YOU REACHED

THE SUMMIT!

Reflections

Reflections